God and You

Romans 1-5

Pete and Anne Woodcock

Series Editor: Tim Chester

The Good Book Company

God and You: the Good Book Guide to Romans 1-5

For Phil
In gratitude and recognition of all
the years he spent working so hard with us.

Published by
The Good Book Company
Tel: 0845-225-0880
Fax: 0845-225-0990
Email: admin@thegoodbook.co.uk
Internet: www.thegoodbook.co.uk

ISBN 1 904889 61 1
ISBN 13: 9781904889618

Printed in the UK

CONTENTS

Read this first!

Every group which gets together to think about the Bible is different. You may be meeting one-to-one or together with other curious 'investigators', or you might be part of a group that studies the Bible regularly. The sessions may take place in a church building, in a home or cafe, on a train, over a leisurely mid-morning coffee or squashed into a 30-minute lunch break. Your group may include mums, students, senior citizens, business people or teenagers. That's why we've designed this course to be flexible for use in many different situations.

Is this the first time you have ever studied the Bible like this? Perhaps you are not really used to looking at a book and discussing it. Don't worry—there are no exams to pass or fail and the course organiser certainly doesn't want to embarrass you in any way. The whole aim of this Good Book Guide is that you will be able to understand the Christian message.

In each session there are three main kinds of question to answer:

Investigate: 'What does it actually say?' It's important that we don't just endlessly discuss our own opinions. If you really want to find out about 'God and you', it's important to know what the Bible actually says. Why the Bible? Well, it's a collection of ancient documents, written over hundreds of years and by many different writers; yet it reads like one book with a single author. It consistently claims that God is the author, and that it is the Word of God. We have included a 'dictionary' in each session that explains any unfamiliar terms.

Think about it: 'Is this true? How does it fit with what we see in the world?' If the Bible really is God's Word to our world, then it's not a collection of fairy tales, or even simply a historical record. What it says must be true and make sense, even to us today.

Getting personal: 'If this this true, then what should we do?' If God is speaking we should be listening and ready to act on what he says to us. These questions are an opportunity for you to think about the changes that you personally may want to make as a result of what you have discovered.

Note: The Leader's Guide contains guidance on questions, and additional 'follow-up' questions, as well as historical background information, explanations of the Bible texts for each session and guidance on how best to help people discover the teaching of the Bible.

Why study *God and You?*

Ask the average person in the street 'What's Christianity all about?' or 'What is a Christian?' you will probably get an answer like 'believing in God' or 'someone who tries to live a good life'. Most people assume that Christians are those who live (or think they live) good lives, following rules that were taught by Jesus. Similarly, most never think of becoming Christians themselves because this way of life seems difficult, or dreary or hypocritical. The problem is that most people have completely misunderstood what real Christianity actually is.

These commonly-held ideas are way off the mark because most people have never got around to seriously looking at what Christianity teaches. Which is why this course has been written. In just six one-hour sessions, *God and You* will introduces you to the central teaching of the Christian message, as it was recorded in the Bible and has been taught throughout the history of the Christian church.

Originally known as Scripture under Scrutiny (SUS), the course was created to explain the Christian message to non-religious university students in Australia. It has since been developed and expanded by Pete and Anne Woodcock for wider use with people of all ages and backgrounds (including those who know nothing about Christianity and have never been to church), in both small groups and one-to-one.

The course is based on part of a letter in the New Testament section of the Bible—Paul's letter to the Christians in Rome (the book known as *Romans*). It's one of 13 letters written by this Jewish rabbi, who became the most famous leader of the early Christian church. Paul had studied the Old Testament (the Jewish scriptures) under the most famous and respected teacher of the day. So when he became a Christian, Paul was uniquely equipped to set down in writing what God has said and done in human history. In Romans, Paul has summarised the entire Christian message—in fact, the message of the whole Bible.

We hope that *God and You* will be a real eye-opener and help you to see, not only how mistaken and negative most popular ideas about Christianity are, but also what fantastic news the message of Jesus Christ is. At the end of this six-week course you may not agree with what you have learned; you may not want to believe the Christian message; but we hope that you will truly understand who Jesus Christ is, and why the message of the Bible is such good news for everyone.

1

Romans chapter 1 v 1-6 and 14-20

SAYS WHO?

talkabout

1. Imagine you go into the home of someone you know nothing about. By looking at the contents and condition of their home, what can (and can't) you find out about them? What added dimension would come from a personal letter written by this person to you?

At the beginning of his letter to the Christians in Rome, Paul sets out who he is—an apostle; he explains what he does—he is 'set apart for the gospel of God' and he calls non-Jewish people to faith, obedience and to belong to Jesus Christ; he gives a summary of the gospel (the good news) of God; he assures these Christians of his love for them; and he tells them why he so wants to visit Rome. We are going to focus on what Paul says about God's message—how people like us can know about God, what we can know about Him and what effect that has on our lives.

investigate

Read Romans 1 v 1-6 & 14-20

DICTIONARY:

apostle = someone who knew all about the life and teaching of Jesus first-hand and was especially chosen by Jesus to teach.

gospel = good news from God.

prophet = someone who brings God's message.

Holy Scriptures = the message of God in written form.

Gentile = anyone who isn't a Jew

righteousness = right in God's eyes

2. According to Paul, what can people know about God? How do they find out about him (see verses 19-20)?

3. In verse 1 Paul mentions the gospel (or message of good news) of God. How has the God of the Bible communicated this message to us?

4. What are the central themes of this message from God? (see v 2-5; v 16-17)

5. Who is God's message for (v 5, 14, 16)?

6. What effect does God's message have on people's lives (v 5, 16)?

7. By what authority does Paul speak (v 1, 9)?

think about it

8. What does God want us to know now? And where do we find this message?

getting personal

- *In what ways might I need to change my view of the Bible?*

- *And of Jesus?*

investigate

9. What did Paul do with the message of God? Why (v 14-16)?

10. What do people do with the truth of God? Why (v 18)?

think about it

11. In what ways do people today 'suppress the truth' about God?

getting personal

- *In what ways am I a 'suppressor of the truth' about God?*
- *What do I need to do in order to be a hearer of the truth about God?*

explore more

Hebrews is another New Testament letter (the author is unknown), written to Jews who had become Christians but who were beginning to question whether it was right to give up the rituals and practices of the Jewish religion.

Read Hebrews 1 v 1-3

- *What do these opening sentences have in common with what we have learned so far from Romans chapter 1?*
- *What else can we learn from these verses?*

2 Romans 1 v 18 – 2 v 1 and 3 v 9-18

WHAT IN THE WORLD ARE WE DOING?

Summary so far:

- God has spoken clearly to this world in the Holy Scriptures, which tell us about Jesus.

talkabout

1. Why is it that sex, scandal and crime always sell books, papers and magazines, and attract the highest viewing rates on television?

investigate

Imagine yourself to be one of the original readers of Paul's letter. One very important fact about you would be whether you had been born a Jew (an ethnic minority in Rome) or a non-Jew (perhaps a Roman, Greek or one of the other numerous ethnic groups that lived in cosmopolitan Rome. 'Gentile' is a name for all non-Jews).

The Jews had a history of thousands of years, recorded in the Old Testament part of the Bible. Throughout their history they had always believed that Israel alone knew and understood the one God of heaven and earth. By contrast, all other ethnic groups were pagan, worshipping many gods by means of man-made idols. Jews believed that by following the law of Moses and the traditions of their elders, they lived in a way that pleased God, and would be rewarded by God; everyone else however was cursed by him. It was not fitting for Jews even to eat with Gentiles, who were considered as worthless as dogs.

A major problem for the Christian church in its early years was that these attitudes sometimes persisted between Christians from Jewish and non-Jewish backgrounds. It's an issue that Paul addresses elsewhere in this letter to Rome.

Read Romans 1 v 18 – 2 v 1

DICTIONARY:
wrath = fierce anger
judgment = condemnation (not discernment)
Gentile = anyone who isn't a Jew
sin = rebellion against God
righteous = right in God's eyes

2. What do we learn about the behaviour and character of the people described in chapter 1?

3. Who are these people? What do you think about them?

4. Who decides what is right and wrong, according to Paul?

5. What does God do about these people? What is surprising about this?

6. Can anyone plead ignorance about God? Why or why not?

7. In chapter 2 verse 1, who is Paul addressing? In what way are these people different from those in chapter 1? In what way are they the same?

8. Why should we not be judgmental?

think about it

9. In what ways are people today judgmental?

getting personal

- *In what ways am I judgmental of others?*
- *What have I learned about myself from these verses?*

investigate

We now fast-forward to chapter 3, where Paul returns to the subject of how people live in this world, and gives his conclusion—a pretty devastating one for Jewish readers. Paul quotes from several writers of the Old Testament (the Jewish scriptures themselves) to prove his point.

Read Romans 3 v 9-18

10. What conclusion does Paul reach in these verses? (Look at the medical check-up that he carries out in verses 13-18—what is the diagnosis?)

think about it

11. Is this true of the world? For example...
- do people worship created things instead of the creator (1 v 25)?
- is everyone a liar (3 v 13)?
- is Paul right when he says that everyone is 'under sin' (3 v 9)?

getting personal

- *What does this say about me?*
- *What follows about my standing with God?*

review

From what we have learned in this session, how can sinful people ever be acceptable to a perfect God?

explore more

Psalms are songs—they were written by a number of different people on a whole variety of themes, sometimes anonymously like this one. They were collected together and used by the people of Israel in praise of God. This collection of songs now forms the book of Psalms in the Old Testament part of the Bible.

Read Psalm 104 v 1-9 and 24-32

- *What does this psalm have in common with what we have learned so far from Romans chapter 1?*
- *What else can we learn from this psalm?*

3

Romans 2 v 1-16

WHAT IN THE WORLD IS GOD DOING?

Summary so far:

- God has spoken clearly to this world in the Holy Scriptures, which tell us about Jesus.
- God is angry because of all the evil and wrong that people do.
- We are wrong to think that other people are bad but we are all right. In fact, we judge ourselves guilty because we do the same things.
- Everyone is guilty of sin.
- God shows his anger by letting us do the wrong things we want to do.
- God's law says that we should die.
- Remember the spiritual check-up (mouth, feet, eyes)

talkabout

1. Do you agree that people should be held responsible and accountable for their actions? What do you think the world would be like if people were not held accountable in any way?

investigate

In this part of his letter, Paul speaks directly to people who have been brought up as God-fearing Jews. They condemn the Gentile pagans around them for their idolatry and wicked lifestyles, never imagining that they themselves are equally guilty and therefore also under God's wrath.

Read Romans 2 v 1-16

DICTIONARY:

righteous = right in God's eyes

unrighteous = not right in God's eyes

the law = the rules God gave to the people of Israel

2. What is God already doing in response to our sinfulness? (Look again at 1 v 18, 24, 26, 28.)

3. What will God do in the future?

4. How will God judge?

- What will he consider?
- Who will do the judging?
- How will he show fairness both to the knowledgeable (the Jews) and the ignorant (the Gentiles)?

think about it

5. Why do you think God judges? Why is he angry about sinfulness?

- Why is this teaching about God's judgment so unpopular today?

- Can God show justice without judgment? Why or why not?

getting personal

- *What does this say about me?*
- *What follows about my standing with God?*

investigate

6. What will happen to the unrighteous? What kind of people are they?

7. What will happen to the righteous? What kind of people are they?

8. How do verses 7-10 fit with Paul's conclusion in 3 v 9-18 (see Session Two, question 10)?

9. How common is the desire for justice in our world?
- Can true justice ever be achieved in this life?
- If there is such a thing as justice in the universe, who can give it, and how?

think about it

10. Do I want God to treat me with justice?

getting personal

- *Do I want God to treat me with justice? No, it's not a printing error, but a second chance to think about this vital question and where it leaves you.*

review

From what we have learned so far, how can anyone be saved from God's wrath and judgment?

explore more

These words of Jesus come in the middle of a famous talk that he gave on the shores of Lake Galilee, witnessed by his disciple Matthew, and known as 'The Sermon on the Mount'.

Matthew records a number of occasions when Jesus spoke about God's judgment and hell, as in these verses.

Read Matthew 5 v 21-22

- *What do these words of Jesus have in common with what we have learned so far from Romans chapter 2?*

- *What else can we learn from them?*

Romans 2 v 17-29 and 3 v 19-20

4 WHAT CAN RELIGION DO?

Summary so far:

- God has spoken clearly to this world in the Holy Scriptures, which tell us about Jesus.
- We are all guilty of sin.
- There is justice in the universe only because one day God will punish all the wrong things that have been done.
- God will punish me for the wrong things I have done and for the wrong secret thoughts that I have had.
- So far, we have found out that the only way to be acceptable to the perfect God is to obey his law. But no one, except Jesus, has done that.

talkabout

1. What do you think is the purpose of religion?

investigate

If you had been brought up as a Jew, the law of Moses would have been central to your way of life. In ancient times, this law had been given by God to the people of Israel, through their leader Moses, after rescue from slavery in Egypt. (You can read about this in the Old Testament book of Exodus.)

The most famous part of this law was the Ten Commandments, but there were also many other rules covering all areas of life, including: religious practices (sacrifices and gifts to God, priests, places of worship, special celebrations); social matters (regulations about marriage, employers, debt etc.); lifestyle regulations (diet, clothing, diseases etc.); and crime and punishment. (You can read about these laws in the Old Testament books of Exodus, Leviticus and Deuteronomy.)

The people of Israel were given this law so that they could show the other nations how great God is and what he does for his people (see Deuteronomy 4 v 5-8). So because of their law, Jews believed that they were a 'light for the Gentiles'.

Read Romans 2 v 17-29

DICTIONARY:

blaspheming = bringing dishonour to the name of God.

circumcision = a minor genital operation performed on Jewish boys as a sign that they were God's people. It was commanded in the law.

the written code = another term for God's law.

2. What does God require of those who have the law? Did the religious people, the Jews, meet those requirements?

3. What was their attitude to the law? Note the verbs used in verses 17, 18, 20, 21 and 23. Was their devotion good enough for God?

4. Who is the condemned law-breaker in verse 27? What would Paul's Jewish readers have made of this?

5. Did circumcision, a religious requirement of Jewish law, make a person right with God?

think about it

6. In our culture, what religious practices have replaced Jewish law and circumcision, as the way by which people think they can be acceptable to God? What similarities are there between our society and these Jews?

getting personal

- *In what ways might I need to change my view of righteousness (ie: goodness that is good enough for God)?*

investigate

Do you remember Paul's conclusion that everyone, Jews and Gentiles alike, are all under sin? We investigated those verses from Romans chapter 3 in Session Two. At the end of that passage, we now find Paul's conclusion about the purpose of Israel's law.

Read Romans 3 v 19-20

7. Will anyone be declared righteous by 'observing the law'?

8. What does the law achieve?

9. Whose law is Paul talking about in these passages? Is there anything wrong with this law?

think about it

10. Can any religious practices (keeping religious rules, performing rituals, having experiences) get you closer to God? Or solve the problem of sin?

getting personal

- *What am I trusting to reconcile me to God? Am I trusting in laws or rituals or experiences to make me righteous?*
- *If so, what are the implications?*

review

From what we have learned so far, is it possible for anyone to be righteous?

explore more

Isaiah was a prophet who lived nearly 800 years before Jesus. Isaiah spoke messages from God mainly to Judah, the smaller of two kingdoms into which Israel had by then divided. Isaiah also prophesied against the surrounding nations, many of whom were threatening Judah. His many prophecies were written down and can be found in the Old Testament book of Isaiah. Some of his prophecies are full of great hope and encouragement for God's people; some, like this one, strongly criticise them for the way they live.

Read Isaiah 1 v 10-17

- *In this passage, what did God think of the Jews' religious practices (many of which were required by the law), and why did he think that?*
- *What do we find in common with what we have learned so far from Romans chapter 2?*
- *What else can we learn from this passage?*

5 Romans 3 v 21-31
GOD'S GIFT

Summary so far:

- God has spoken clearly to this world in the Holy Scriptures, which tell us about Jesus.
- We are all guilty of sin.
- There is justice in the universe only because one day God will punish all wrong things that have been done.
- God will punish me for the wrong things that I have done and for the wrong secret thoughts that I have had.
- Even God's law can't make us right with him, because no one can keep God's law. God's law only shows us our sin.

talkabout

1. Imagine that you unexpectedly receive a very generous and much needed gift, given purely out of love and kindness? How do you feel towards the giver? In what way is this different to receiving a payment, right or reward? Can you think of reasons why people sometimes dislike receiving gifts?

investigate

2. Who will be declared righteous in God's sight, according to Paul, (look at 3 v 9, 10, 20)?

If you were a Jew reading Paul's letter, you would probably be feeling quite confused by the end of chapter 2. After all, for hundreds of years God had sent prophets to the nation of Israel to remind them that they were his specially chosen people with unique privileges. But, as we've already seen, Paul writes that, when it comes to God's judgment, there is no difference between a Jew and a non-Jew.

So what's the advantage in being a Jew? This is the question that Paul answers in chapter 3, verses 1-8. But then he still comes to the same conclusion—Jews and Gentiles alike are all under sin (v 9-18—see Session Two) and the law can't help anyone, not even Jews, to become good enough for God (v 19-20—see Session Four). If even God's people, the Jews, with God's law, cannot be declared righteous and cannot escape his wrath on the Day of Judgment, what hope is there for anyone?

No hope! We have reached the point where we must realise that there is NOTHING we can do to save ourselves. (Look again at the Review questions at the end of Sessions Two, Three and Four and check out your answers.) But the night seems darkest just before dawn. Finally, we are ready to hear the good news.

Read Romans 3 v 21-31

DICTIONARY:

the Law and the Prophets = God's Word to Israel, now two major sections of the Old Testament

faith = trust, dependence;

justified = to be declared right

grace = undeserved favour

redemption = paying the price to free a slave

atonement= making amends for wrong, leading to reconciliation

forbearance = mercy to sinners

3. Based on verses 21-26, write out in your own words how someone can become right with God. (To help you, think about the following questions.)

- **v 21-22:** What do people need to be reconciled to God? Where does it come from and where does it not come from? How do we get this?
- **v 24:** Look at the word 'justified'. What does God think of people who have faith in Jesus Christ?
- **v 24:** Look at the words 'freely by his grace'. Do we have a right to expect that God must do this? Do we earn it or pay for it?
- **v 24:** Look at the word 'redemption'. What 'price' did Jesus Christ pay? What 'slavery' does this free us from?

- **v 25:** Look at the words 'sacrifice of atonement'. What was the significance of Jesus' death?
- **v 25:** What do we need to trust in to get right with God?

4. How can Jesus' death pay for our sin?

5. How can the crucifixion of Jesus demonstrate God's justice (v 25)?

think about it

6. How can God be both merciful and just at the same time?

- Is there any other way in which God can show that he is both just and merciful?

- How does the good news of Jesus Christ fit with today's popular belief that there are many ways to God?

getting personal

- *In what ways might I need to change my views of other teachings about how we can be acceptable to God?*

investigate

7. Is this gift of righteousness from God deserved?

8. Who receives the gift, and how do they receive it?

9. Does a Christian (someone who has been made right with God through Jesus Christ) have any reason for boasting (verses 27-28)? Or for being judgmental?

think about it

10. Is anyone too sinful for God to forgive them? Why or why not?

getting personal

- *Am I too sinful to be acceptable to God based on my own goodness?*
- *Am I too sinful to be acceptable to God based on Jesus' death?*
- *Where does my faith lie? In Jesus' death or in something else?*
- *What would it mean for me to put my faith in Jesus' death?*

pray

At this stage in the course, you may have reached the point where you understand the gospel of God. If you are now ready to put your faith in Jesus Christ, and ask him to save you from your sin and God's judgment, all you need to do is to talk to God about it. In your own time and your own words, you can say a prayer like the one below. If you truly mean what you say to God, you can be confident that he will hear and answer your prayer.

Dear God,
I know that I have lived as your enemy.

Thank you that you love me anyway and sent Jesus to die on my behalf.

Please forgive me and change me so that I may live with Jesus as my Lord.

explore more

The Exodus was one of the most famous and important events in the history of Israel. The Jews had been enslaved in the land of Egypt, where they suffered terribly. But God chose Moses to approach Pharaoh, the ruler of Egypt, and present him with God's command—to let God's people, the Jews, leave. Each time Moses visited, Pharaoh would refuse, so God would send a plague on Egypt—a judgment on Pharaoh for his stubborn disobedience. This culminated in one final plague—the death of every firstborn in Egypt.

Read Exodus 12 v 1-13

- *How were the people of Israel saved from God's judgment on Egypt?*

Later, after the escape from Egypt, God gave Israel his law through Moses, specifying how the people of Israel were to approach God for forgiveness or thanksgiving, by means of animal sacrifices. The blood of the dead animal made it possible for sinners to approach God, and yet not be destroyed. Isaiah uses this picture of a sacrificial lamb in one of his most famous prophecies about God's promised chosen servant (the Messiah).

Read Isaiah 53 v 4-12

- *What happens to God's servant and why?*

Read John 1 v 29

- *What does John tell us about Jesus?*

- *What do these passages have in common with what we have learned so far?*

6 Romans 5 v 1-11

RIGHT WITH GOD

Summary so far:

- God has spoken clearly to this world in the Holy Scriptures, which tell us about Jesus.
- We are all guilty of sin.
- There is justice in the universe only because one day God will punish all the wrong things that have been done.
- God will punish me for the wrong things that I have done and for the wrong secret thoughts that I have had.
- Even God's law can't make us right with him, because no one can keep God's law. God's law only shows us our sin.
- BUT God has a way to make people right with him, not by trying to keep the law but by faith in Jesus Christ and the significance of his death.
- Jesus died as a sacrifice of atonement, which means he took my place and suffered the penalty for sin that is required before reconciliation with God can occur.
- If I trust in Jesus and what he did on the cross, God will declare me 'Not Guilty' and I will not be punished on the day of judgment.

talkabout

1. What is the most striking example of reconciliation you have had with another person in your life, or know of in someone else's life? Or give an example from history.

investigate

Paul has just dropped a bombshell for his readers: no one will be saved from God's judgment by trying to keep religious laws or perform religious rituals—not even Jews trying to keep God's law. We cannot be saved by anything that we do; we can only be saved by faith (trust) in what Jesus has done for us.

Jewish readers were going to take some convincing about this, so in chapter 4, Paul shows that, way back at the beginning of Israel's long history, even Abraham, the 'father' of the Jews, had been justified (declared righteous) through faith, because he believed God, not because of anything that he had done.

Paul has shown us clearly how God, who is both merciful and just, can make us righteous. But, if by putting faith in Jesus Christ, we accept this incredible gift, what difference will that make in our lives?

Read Romans 5 v 1-11

2. List the benefits of being a Christian mentioned in the passage; in the past, the present and the future.

Past	Present	Future

think about it

3. What do you think it would be like to be at peace with God? How would your thinking change? How would your life change?

getting personal

- *In my search for God, have I got to the stage where I can say I am at peace with God?*
- *Would I like to be reconciled to God?*

investigate

4. By what means do Christians gain access to God's grace, so that they can now receive his love and kindness, instead of his wrath and judgment?

5. Does suffering in this life mean that people are not right with God? Why or why not?

6. Why do you think Christians are expected to suffer (v 3-5)?

7. How has God demonstrated his love? So how do we know that God loves us even when we are suffering?

8. What will Christians be saved from?

9. What assurances does Paul give us that the problem of sin really has been dealt with, and therefore Christians will be saved on the day of judgment? (See chapters 4 v 25 and 5 v 9-10.)

think about it

10. What right do you think Christians have to be sure that they are going to heaven?

getting personal

- *Am I absolutely sure that when I die my body will be raised to enjoy eternal life with the God who loves me in his perfect new universe? Why or why not?*

explore more

This course ends in chapter five of Paul's letter to the Romans, but the letter goes on, packed with amazing and important teaching for Christians. This is a very famous section that has been loved, quoted and memorised by innumerable Christians through the ages.

Read Romans 8 v 28-39

- *What do these verses teach in common with what we have learned so far from Romans chapter five?*
- *What else can we learn from this passage?*

conclusion

As a result of what you have learned on this course, what do you think you need to do now?

Leader's Guide: Introduction

So you're about to lead a group of people through this *God and You* Bible study. This may be the first time that some of your group have ever studied the Bible in this way, so you will need to:

- **welcome** guests and if necessary introduce each person.
- **reassure people** that they will not be made to do anything embarrassing or religious—singing, praying or reading aloud.
- **don't assume anything.** It really is worth explaining everything briefly—what the letter to the Romans is, the background of the letter and who Paul was (See *Why study God and You?* at the front of the Study Guide.)
- **explain the system of chapter and verses of the Bible**— large numbers in the Bible denoting chapters and small numbers indicating verses. There is no reason why 'first-timers' will know this.
- **explain the format of each session,** including the different types of questions, and the icons in the Study Guide (See *Read this first!* on page 4 of the Study Guide.)

THE ROLE OF THE LEADER: Explain your role as the leader. You are not here to preach but to lead the group through the passage to discover what the Bible really says. So you will need to keep asking questions like: 'Where in the passage does it say that?'

ENCOURAGING DISCUSSION:
Encourage people to feel free to speak without fear of looking stupid. You can say something like: 'Lets imagine this group is a brain and each of us are different brain cells. If someone says something not quite right, it may actually help other 'cells' to see the correct answer. So all contributions can help the 'brain' as a whole to function correctly.' Explain that some people might have strong disagreements but that can be very healthy and make us think. We can disagree without being disagreeable.

HOW THIS COURSE WORKS: Explain that *God and You* is a course that builds up like a bricklayer building a wall. If you only see the foundations you might not be impressed with how wonderful the final building will be. But if you miss the foundations then the building will collapse. Encourage people to come to all the sessions.

Explain that Sessions 2-4 are the **bad news**, but people shouldn't give up at that point or they will miss the good news. You can make a bit of a joke about this, 'What do you want first—the good news or the bad news? Well, here we have the bad news first!' Another helpful illustration is that of a jeweller who shows off his prize diamond by placing it on black velvet. The blackness shows how beautiful the diamond is. Similarly, we will never fully appreciate the remarkably beautiful good news of the Bible without the contrast of the bad news first.

USING THE STUDY GUIDE
Your Bible-study group is unique, and you are likely to know better than anyone the capabilities, backgrounds and circumstances of the people you are leading. That's why we've designed these guides with a number of optional features. If they're a silent bunch you might want to spend longer on **talkabout**. If they start to enjoy Bible study there are optional **explore more** homework projects at the end of each session. As leader, you can adapt and select the material to the needs of your particular group. So let's take a look at the various different features of this course.

Summary: sessions 2-6 begin with a summary of the main points of all the previous sessions. Sometimes it may be helpful to get the participants to recap themselves before going through the summary together.

talkabout: each session kicks off with a discussion question, based on the group's opinions or experiences. It's designed to get people talking and thinking in a general way about the main subject of the Bible study.

investigate: these questions help people to discover what the Bible actually says. If you read the questions out before reading the Bible passage, people will know what to look out for. Watch out for answers that don't refer to the Bible passage at all. It's amazing how often we can get through a Bible study without actually looking at the Bible! The Leader's Guide contains guidance on questions. These are the answers to which you need to direct your group. This information isn't meant to be read out to people—ideally, you want them to discover these answers from the Bible for themselves. Sometimes optional follow-up questions (see in guidance on questions) are included, to help you help your group get to the answer. Note: when reading the Bible it is best either to read it yourself or have someone you have asked earlier. Some people find reading aloud very frightening.

think about it: these questions encourage people to consider what the Bible teaching says about us and to us today. getting personal can be done at home, or you could allocate a few moments of quiet reflection for each person to think about their response to the Bible teaching. This is a crucial part of the course. We do Bible study so that our lives can be changed by what we hear and understand in God's Word. If you skip these sections the Bible study won't achieve its purpose.

review: some sessions end with a question that summarises the 'progress of the investigation'. These questions are vital for driving home the truth about our relationship with God.

USING THE LEADER'S GUIDE

The Leader's Guide will help you to understand the major teaching points in the passage you are studying, and how to apply them. As well as guidance on questions, the Leader's Guide for each session contains the following important sections:

the big idea: one key sentence gives you the main point of the session. This is what you should be aiming to have fixed in people's minds as they leave the Bible study. And it's the point you need to head back towards when the discussion goes off at a tangent.

the issues: various points outlining problems and pitfalls that may arise from the session, with helpful theological information and illustrations to deal with them.

summary: an overview of the passage, including plenty of useful historical background information.

pray: although your group will not be expected to pray themselves, you may want to lead with a closing prayer. This section gives a relevant Bible passage on which to base a prayer of response to what has been learned.

For further help and ideas in setting up a *God and You* course, or in training people to lead a *God and You* course, visit the Good Book Company website, where a free downloadable guide and training course is available.
www.thegoodbook.co.uk

1 Romans 1 v 1-6 and 14-20

SAYS WHO?

THE BIG IDEA

God has spoken to our world through creation, but above all, through Jesus his Son, as recorded in the Holy Scriptures (the Bible), so we must listen.

THE ISSUES

1. This session sets the scene for the following five sessions, by showing that God's communication culminates in Jesus. This shows where the course will eventually get us to, which hopefully, will encourage people to hang in through three sessions of bad news.

2. Because this session is about God communicating, you might find that people have strange mystical ideas of how and what God communicates. People often think of something like fortune-telling when they hear about God speaking, but we need to realise that God's message is universal in its scope, and bigger and more important than the small events of our individual lives.

3. You will see that this session covers two forms of communication from God:

- **Natural revelation:** God revealing himself through what we see in our universe.
- **Special revelation:** God speaking through prophets, whose words are written down in Scripture. So what we see in nature should move us to ask how we can find out about God, and what he wants us to do.

SUMMARY

At the beginning of his letter to Christians in Rome, Paul introduces his readers to the gospel (good news) of God—the message for which he himself has been set apart (v 1), to 'call people from among all the Gentiles, to the obedience that comes from faith' (v 5). This means that our Creator has spoken—clearly. Our responsibility is to listen to what God is saying.

Paul tells us where to find this message—by reading the words of prophets in the Holy Scriptures ie: the Old Testament (v 2), and in the life of Jesus (v 3-4). He tells us what this message is about—Jesus Christ, the human descendant of King David who, through the Holy Spirit, has been shown to be the Son of God (v 3-4). He tells us what this message can do in the lives of people—'it is the power of God for the salvation of everyone who believes' (v 16) and it reveals a righteousness from God that is by faith (v 17).

The implications for us are that God wants us to learn about Jesus Christ, by reading the Holy Scriptures—the writings of the prophets in the Old Testament, and in the New Testament, the writings of the apostles, like Paul, who were called to preach this message (v 9). But the purpose of this good news is not just that we learn about Jesus; God wants us to believe, so that we can be saved, and receive from God his righteousness (v 16-17). What we need to be saved from, and why we need God's righteousness are questions that will be answered in subsequent sessions.

Finally, Paul tells us that all humans know some truth about God, simply because we live in the universe he has created (v 19-20). However, the human response is to suppress truth about God because of our wickedness (v 18).

The challenge of this session is to make us consider how we personally may be guilty of suppressing God's truth, and what we need to do in order to hear and obey God.

GUIDANCE ON QUESTIONS

1.

- **Think of as many ways of communicating as possible. What kind of communication tends to be the most accurate, and the least likely to be corrupted or open to different interpretations?**
Words, rather than physical gestures, pictures or symbols; and written words rather than spoken ones.

This question draws out the distinction between natural and special revelation—the difference between what I know about someone, and how I can know (or relate to) that person.

Note: sources of information about the person should not include anything written by them, as the point being made is that it is written communication that reveals so much more of a person than pictures and objects in their home.
Many things can be discovered about a person by looking around their home—age, occupation, current marital and family status, family and educational background, interests and hobbies, standards of living and hygiene, state of health etc. Without written communication it will be difficult, if not impossible, to work out a person's opinions, morality, intelligence, expectations of other people, and traits such as willingness to forgive—in other words, most aspects of their thinking and character. A letter would be able to reveal these things and also allow you to understand what kind of relationship you could have with this person.

2. According to Paul, because everyone lives in the created universe, everyone knows that there is a God, with divine nature and eternal power (v 19-20).
We know that somewhere in the universe there is someone who is utterly different to us and unimaginably more powerful than us, who has made everything we can see and know about.
So what about atheists? It's worth considering for a few moments just how complex and finely-tuned the universe is, and how narrow the margins are within which life can be sustained on earth.
How rational is it to believe that something spontaneously came from nothing, that systems and structures of such incredible design and delicate balance were the result of chance accidents, or that life and consciousness suddenly came from non-living substances? Actually, atheism requires far more faith than belief in a creator God!

- **Can people learn everything about God from the created universe?** No, the things that are clearly seen are God's invisible qualities of eternal power and divine nature (v 20)—ie: God's 'Godness'. Living in God's created universe is like learning about someone simply from visiting their home; it can't tell us everything about God.

3. Through his prophets in the Holy Scriptures (v 2) —ie: in the Old Testament. Also through the teaching of apostles like Paul (v 9), which has been written down and now forms the New Testament part of the Bible. Verses 2-4 (see also Hebrews 1 v 1-2 in Explore More below) show a progression of promises, prophecies and historical events, culminating in the life, death and resurrection of Jesus.

4.

• **What can we find out about Jesus from Paul's introductory summary of the gospel?** He is human, descended from Israel's King David (v 3); his coming was promised by prophets in the Old Testament (v 2); he is the Son of God (v 4); he was shown to be the Son of God by the Spirit's power at work in him (v 4); he was resurrected from the dead, which proves he is the Son of God (v 4); he is Lord (v 4); through him Paul received grace (God's undeserved kindness) (v 5); people like Paul are his servants (v 1), and their job is to call people, even non-Jews, to obey him (v 5); all people, not just Jews, should belong to him (v 6).

The gospel of God is all about his Son (v 3), Jesus Christ our Lord (v 4). Other key themes are obedience and faith (v 5), the salvation of everyone who believes (v 16), and a righteousness from God that is by faith (v 17).

5. God's message is for everyone (v 5, 14, 16).

6. God's message saves everyone who believes (v 16), and brings them into a life of obedience (v 5) and belonging to Jesus Christ (v 6).

7. Paul speaks with the authority of God. This message is not his own idea—he calls it 'the gospel of God' (v 1) and 'the gospel of His Son' (v 9). Paul is not a free agent—he calls himself a servant of Jesus Christ (v 1) and of God (v 9), and he serves them by preaching their good news.

8. Think about it: People have many different ideas of how God speaks to them (dreams, coincidences, voices in their heads) and what he speaks about (usually guidance in relation to some personal decision eg: career, relationships, where to live). But according to Paul, the key thing that God wants us to know about is His Son, Jesus Christ; the place where we find this message is the Bible, which includes the writings of the prophets (Old Testament) and the teaching of the apostles (New Testament). If we neglect to read the Bible, or if we read it for 'messages' other than the good news of Jesus Christ, we will fail to hear God's message to us.
It is vital to understand that the only thing God has to say to us, while we are still his enemies, is that we need to be rescued through Jesus.

9. Paul devoted his whole life to preaching God's message (v 9). He aimed to see people's lives changed as they put faith in God's Son and began to live obediently (v 5). This was because, through Jesus Christ, Paul himself had received grace from God. He was then called by God to be an apostle (someone specially chosen to teach the gospel) (v 5). He felt he had to preach this message to everyone (v 14), but it wasn't just a dull duty—he was also eager to do it (v 15)! He knew in his own life the power of the gospel to save and so, despite the opposition and hatred of his fellow Jews, he was unashamed of the good news of Jesus Christ (v 16).

10. People suppress the truth of God, because they are wicked (v 18).

11. Think about it: There are many ways in which the truth about God can be suppressed; for example:

- by claiming that anything to do with God is a matter of faith, which can't be proved right or wrong, and therefore can't be truth—whereas science, because it is 'testable', can give us truth. Because science cannot prove God, it's not reasonable to believe in him.
- by making sure that any reference to God is kept out of public life (eg: state schools, politics, local government funded events etc.), for fear of 'offending religious minorities'.
- by viewing the Bible as a great work of literature, rather than a message from God that we must respond to.
- by using the failures of Christians as a reason not to investigate the gospel.
- by keeping Bible stories, Christmas etc. for children.
- by keeping 'religious stuff' for old age.

Group members should have their own ideas about how people suppress the truth about God.

PRAY

Think carefully about how you lead a final prayer. The idea of praying to God might be quite new for some people. The key is not to embarrass anyone, or make them feel under pressure. Keep it simple, short and to the point of what you have discovered in this study.

'This is the confidence we have in approaching God: that if we ask anything according to his will, he hears us'

1 John 5 v 14

Think about the following questions to guide you in closing the session with a prayer.

- What have we learned about what God wants?
- What can we pray for 'according to his will'?

EXPLORE MORE

Explain to the group that at the end of the study, there is an optional piece of 'homework' they can do if they want. Encourage them to do it on their own, and offer to discuss it at the start of the next meeting.

What's the same?

- Previously, God spoke through prophets.
- God now speaks to us through his Son.
- God's Son is powerful.

What else do we learn?

- God's Son has been appointed as his heir.
- God made the universe through his Son.
- God's Son shows us what God is like, exactly and gloriously.
- God's Son sustains everything.
- He provided purification for sins.
- He sits in heaven at God's right hand.

2 Romans 1 v 18 - 2 v 1 and 3 v 9-18
WHAT IN THE WORLD ARE WE DOING?

THE BIG IDEA

Everyone is a sinner and God is rightly angry at sin.

THE ISSUES

1. Is there a scale to sin? It is vital that we understand the truth that everyone alike has rejected God ('suppress the truth' – v 18) and consequently, God is acting in a wrathful way towards us. In this, there is no scale of sinfulness. Paul clearly argues that whatever people have done that is wrong, it all started with a rejection of God. Part of God's response is to actively make people face the consequences of this rejection ('...gave them over...'—v 24, 26, 28). As we read through the passage it will become clear that we cannot claim innocence when it comes to gossip, slander, disobeying parents etc.

2. Isn't homosexuality natural? Does God hate homosexuals? Questions like these may well arise in the minds of westerners, although strange to say, they are generally not expressed. This topic will normally not be raised at all by those from non-western cultures, where the practice is still largely seen as unnatural. Paul would be contradicting himself if he were highlighting homosexuality as the 'worst' sin. Instead, he highlights it because it was a common practice in Roman society, and is a good example of how far people have moved from God in their actions. The major issue here is who has the right to decide what is right or wrong. If it is God who has this right, then what seems natural or unnatural to us makes no difference—God is the one to say. This is best for us since otherwise everyone will have their own idea of what is right and wrong. The paedophile and the liar will each justify their actions as being natural and/or reasonable.
So, without a standard of truth from outside our own opinions, how would we know what is right?

SUMMARY

Although Paul refers to God's message as the gospel or good news, he is about to tell us some very bad news. In fact, the next three sessions of this course deal exclusively with bad news. Paul is in the same position as a doctor—he needs to diagnose and explain the problem to his patient before he can give the good news of the treatment.

In the first part of chapter one, Paul has introduced us to the fact that God has a message for this world, and from verse 18, he starts to tell us God's message. The first thing that we need to know from God is that he is angry at the wickedness of human beings; the rest of chapter one describes the extent of this wickedness in great detail.

It starts with people clearly understanding that there is a God, and something of what he is like, but suppressing that knowledge (v 18), refusing to treat him as God (v 21), and turning instead to idolatry (v 23). In his wrath, God's response is to give people over to the wicked things that they want to do.

So begins a terrible downward spiral into worse and worse wrongdoing (v 24-32).

How would Paul's Christian readers, particularly those brought up as Jews, have reacted to this catalogue of wickedness? Jews would have been brought up to hate idolatry, sexual immorality and the excesses of this kind of pagan living. Probably they would have 'tut tutted' their condemnation of these people, and nodded their approval of God's wrath against them. But they are in for a shock! Suddenly, Paul starts to address his readers directly (2 v 1) and he seems to know just how they (and we) are reacting. But instead of commending us for our superior 'goodness', Paul tells us that, at the very moment we condemn others, we are condemning ourselves (2 v 1). The reason is that we all do the same things—we are all under sin (3 v 9-18).

The challenge of this session is to see that there is no such thing as 'good' people, but that we are all sinners. We are in the same situation as those people that we consider bad. We are all equally under God's wrath.

GUIDANCE ON QUESTIONS

1. Humans have a fascination with bad behaviour. Perhaps we would like to do something similar, but we don't have the guts to go through with it. Or we enjoy a sense of superiority, because we seem to be better than the people we see or read about. Anyone can feel they are a saint when compared to an out-and-out criminal.

2. Though the truth about God is plain to these people (v 19), from the fact that they live in a universe of intelligent design (v 20), they suppress that truth (v 18). This means that they refuse to treat God like God (v 21), and worship idols instead (v 23). God's response is to give them over to their sinful desires ie: he allows them to do whatever sinful things they want to do (v 24). This leads to sexual impurity (v 24), homosexuality—which overturns the gender distinctions that God has created—(v 26-27), a depraved mind (v 28), and evil behaviour affecting every aspect of life, including both the worst of crimes (murder—v 29) and indiscretions so common that we believe they are just normal behaviour (envy and gossip—v29). Finally, these people go on to invent further ways of doing evil (v 30), they continue to do things that they know deserve God's penalty of death, and they also approve of anyone else who does such things (v 32).

The passage naturally encourages people to think in terms of 'them' and 'us'. You get the sense that Paul is trying to provoke a reaction of disgust towards these people, using extreme examples like homosexuality. Today, we might talk about paedophiles instead. It's important to feel this, because it reflects our natural way of thinking. Later, (see questions 7 and 8), Paul twists around and points the finger back at self-righteous people. At this point, it would be good to go back over the list of behaviours in chapter 1, read them out individually and ask ourselves which ones we are guilty of.

3. At the time when Paul wrote this letter, it would have been clear to his readers that he was describing Roman society; the Romans worshipped many gods, homosexuality was openly practised and the imperial capital was notorious for the bad behaviour of its citizens. For these reasons, all Jews would have looked down on Romans. It would be interesting to discuss which groups of people in our society provoke a similar reaction.

4. This question can be answered in two ways from the passage; God, who has the right to decide what is right and wrong, or humans, who have seized that right. From this we can see how man is actually trying to be God. Notice that when Paul says (v 32) that it is God who decides what is right and wrong, he doesn't come up with any reasons why this is so—he simply states the fact. God is angry at the wickedness of humans (v 18); there is no question of debating whether he is right to be angry. People are inexcusably foolish to worship created things rather than the Creator (v 21-23); there is no possibility that their behaviour could be valid. It is God's right to decide what is right and wrong, simply because he is God; it is not our right to do so, simply because we are not God.

5. God gives these people over to their wickedness (v 24, 26, 28); ie: he lets them get on with it. This may seem surprising because we generally think that if God is angry at a particular behaviour, he will stop it. However according to Paul, God lets us do these things, not because of a 'relaxed attitude', but rather, to show his wrath. Therefore, we should never think that just because God hasn't prevented us from doing something, he doesn't really mind how we live.

6. No one can plead ignorance about God, because he has made the truth about himself plain to everyone (v 18-20). But people may argue that God hasn't made himself equally plain to everyone...

- **What about those who have never heard about God?** (This is dealt with in Romans chapter 2, see Session 3.) Verse 20 focuses on seeing/experiencing creation, rather than hearing God's Word, as the thing by which we are judged to have 'no excuse'. Since all humans are born into the universe that God created, all can understand that there is a God, simply by experiencing what he has made.
- **What about those, who, because of mental incapacity or death in infancy, never have the opportunity to think through these issues?** Here we have to trust in a God who is good, loves the world and cannot be limited in how he communicates to his creation. 'Will not the judge of all the earth do right?' The problem is, we don't trust God in these areas because we don't really know him. So we need to encourage ourselves to keep on learning about God.

Be careful not to let this discussion dominate the session. Most people will prefer to discuss about other people and their lack of knowledge. The big challenge, that we must help group members to see, is that those of us who *have* understood, will have no excuse at all!

7. In chapter 2 v 1, Paul changes from speaking about 'they' and 'them' to 'you'. He is addressing the Christians in Rome, who would be the first to read his letter. Many of these Christians were ethnically Jewish. The people addressed in chapter 2 are different from those described in chapter 1 because they do not approve of their wickedness, but rather, condemn it. To pass judgment like this, these people must feel that they are above such behaviour. However, they are the same as the people they judge because, Paul says, they do the same things.

8. See 2 v 1. We should not pass judgment on others because we actually do the same things, and so judge ourselves guilty as well.

9. Think about it: Judgmentalism is universal, and it's not just religious people who are judgmental. For instance: a vegetarian can be judgmental about the diet of non-vegetarians, and yet wear leather shoes; parents can be judgmental about the failings of other parents, and yet be blind to their own failings; a politician may rant against declining family values, while at the same time they are secretly having an affair; we 'tut' at what we see on television, but we regularly tune in to watch etc. Group members will have their own examples of judgmentalism.

10. See 3 v 9. Jew and Gentiles alike (ie: everyone) are under sin. It's likely that some people will have a problem with the following statements—'No one seeks God' (3 v 11); 'there is no one who does good' (3 v 12); 'Their feet are swift to shed blood' (3 v 15).

- **'No one seeks God'.** What about sincere Buddhists/Muslims etc? The crucial point is that they are not seeking the God of the Bible, but a false god. A helpful illustration is of someone who misses meeting you at an airport because they have a false idea of what you look like. They see you but they walk straight past. Religion can be one of the best hiding places from God.
- **'There is no one who does good'.** Jesus excepted, of course! A Bible definition of good is to 'love the Lord your God with all your heart, soul, mind and strength, and to love your neighbour as yourself' (see Matthew 22 v 36-40). If you don't love God, you can't truly love your neighbour. The reason we don't do good is because we don't seek God. Instead, we seek to justify ourselves by doing what we think is good, and limiting our goodness to human standards and ideas. No one loves God with all their heart, soul, mind and strength, so therefore, according to the Bible, no one does good.
- **'Their feet are swift to shed blood'.** Well, surely you only need to look at the history of humans. Wherever people have gone in this world, there has been anger, violence and bloodshed. Note that Paul gives a spiritual check-up in 3 v 9-18, in which he looks at our mouths (tongues), feet and eyes. Our mouths produce words full of deadly poisonous deceit, cursing and bitterness (v 13-14); wherever our feet take us, we leave a trail of ruin and misery (v 15-17); there is no fear of God before our eyes (v 18). A useful summarising question for the beginning of next session would be: 'Can anyone remember the diagnosis from the spiritual check-up?'

11. Think about it: This question is an opportunity for the group to discuss whether Paul's statements fit with their experience of the world.

REVIEW

This passage tells us how people ought to be acceptable to God—they should accept the plain truth about God that has been revealed to them, by glorifying him as God and by giving thanks to him. But, what we have learned from this session is that we have all failed to do this and, regardless of whether we consider ourselves 'good' or 'bad', we are all alike under sin. There is nothing in this session that tells us how sinful people like us can become acceptable to God. However, people can be encouraged by the reminder that good news is coming.

PRAY

'O my God, I am too ashamed and disgraced to lift up my face to you, my God, because our sins are higher than our heads and our guilt has reached to the heavens...What has happened to us is a result of our evil deeds and our great guilt, and yet, our God, you have punished us less than our sins have deserved...Here we are before you in our guilt, though because of it not one of us can stand in your presence.' **Ezra 9 v 6, 13, 15**

Think about the following questions to guide you in closing the session with a prayer.

- How should we come to God when we pray to him?
- What should we pray for?

EXPLORE MORE

What's the same?

- God is the creator of the universe.
- His power and nature can be seen from what has been made.

What else do we learn?

- God is unimaginably awesome.
- God is in complete control of what he has made.
- Every living thing depends utterly on God for food and life.

3 Romans 2 v 1-16
WHAT IN THE WORLD IS GOD DOING?

THE BIG IDEA

God is the righteous judge and one day will judge all sin.

THE ISSUES

This session highlights people's desire to see justice done—without it there is anarchy. Yet we are presented with the 'Catch-22' that if, in the pursuit of justice, evil is to be wiped out from the face of the earth, then we too must all be wiped out. People easily forget the conclusions of last session, about how God views our sinfulness, so this may need to be pointed out and explained again.

SUMMARY

The bad news of the last session gets worse! Not only is everyone a sinner and now under God's wrath (Session 2), but one day, God will judge everything that we do (2 v 6); in fact, even the things that we only secretly think about, and haven't yet carried out, will be judged (v 16).

In comparison with our evil judgment of others (2 v 1), God's judgment is... **based on truth** (v 2); **personal**—people are accountable for their own actions, not those of others (v 6); **fair and impartial** (v 11-15); **comprehensive**—nothing that we have done, not even our most secret deeds, will escape his judgment (v16).

God will reward with eternal life those 'who by persistence in doing good seek glory, honour and immortality' (v 7), but he will punish with trouble and distress all those 'who are self-seeking and who reject the truth and follow evil' (v 8). It seems that God will divide everyone into one of two groups, 'good' or 'bad', and this fits very naturally with the way in which most people think. But it doesn't fit with what we have already learned in Session 2, especially Paul's conclusion about people in Romans 3 v 9-18—that everyone, without exception, is a sinner. (see the notes on question 6 below).

This historic Christian teaching of a Day of Judgment has become increasingly unpopular in our generation. Discomfort with this teaching is felt even by those who profess to be Bible-believing Christians. Yet in all cultures, people continue to expect and seek justice from God. The challenge of this session is to understand that God can only be just because he judges. God is just, and so all of us are destined to be judged by him.

GUIDANCE ON QUESTIONS

2. God is giving people over to their sinful desires, shameful lusts and depraved minds—he is letting people get on with sin and get deeper into sin.

3. God will judge us (see verses 2, 3, 5-11, 12 and 16) on the day of his wrath (v 5).

4. In answering this question, find everything that you can about God as judge—that he's fair (v 11), that his judgment is not based on emotion but on truth (v 2), that he judges each person for their own deeds (v 6) rather than for those of their parents, or children or the government etc.

Has anyone in the group been on a jury or in a court? Wouldn't it be fantastic to have judges and juries like this? — someone who knows absolutely what you have or haven't done, and what people's true motives are. We are such poor judges—we can be prejudiced simply by the way someone speaks or dresses. You only have to think of how often good parents make wrong judgments about their own children.

- God will consider what each person has done and he will also judge men's secrets (v 16) ie: those things that we haven't done, but wanted to do or thought about doing.
- God will judge us through Jesus Christ. (See follow-up question below.)
- This question again raises the issue of those who have never heard about God. There are two things to say here. 1. The Bible tells us that everyone in the world who experiences creation has knowledge of God. 2. This passage tells us that everyone has a God-given conscience to guide them. So the problem is not that people have no knowledge, but that they suppress the truth and ignore their conscience. Those who have the law will be judged by what the law says (v 12-13), whereas those who do not have the law will be judged by their consciences (v 14-15).

- **What can we learn about the man Jesus Christ from the fact that he is the one who will judge us (compare 2 v 1)?** Jesus has never committed any sin, otherwise he would be unable to judge us.

5. Think about it: Possible answers may include: because God is holy and therefore hates sin; because God controls everything and therefore will not let evil win; because God passionately loves his creation and therefore is angered at the hurt and damage which sin causes; because God is just and therefore determined to see that justice is done.

- Our society values personal freedom and autonomy, and is suspicious of authority, so the idea that someone else (even God) can tell us what to do or not to do is offensive. Any idea of universal moral standards has mostly been rejected in favour of personal values ie: as a rule, each person can do what is right in his/her own eyes. The idea of guilt has largely disappeared. Instead it is believed that people act 'inappropriately' because they are victims of their genetic make-up, or their up-bringing, or prejudice; therefore, it is thought that wrongdoers should be helped rather than punished. The Christian teaching about God's judgment runs counter to all these popular beliefs.
- Without judgment, a wrongdoer never pays for the pain they have caused their victim. The victim suffers all the pain and cost through no fault of their own, while the wrongdoer, with whom all the fault lies, suffers no pain or cost. Clearly, that is unjust. There can only be justice for victims if wrongdoers are judged—it is impossible to have justice without judgment. Someone may object that God can do the impossible. However, as C.S. Lewis said, God can do miracles, but not nonsense. 'Nonsense remains nonsense even if we talk it about God.'

6. Note that the questions deal first with the unrighteous and secondly, with the righteous, rather than following the order

in the Bible passage, to allow the apparent contradiction between what Paul says about the righteous in v 6, and his conclusion in 3 v 9-18, to be discussed in question 7.
The unrighteous will receive wrath and anger (v 8), trouble and distress (v 9). The unrighteous are those who are self-seeking, who reject the truth and follow or do evil (v 8-9).

- **Who is self-seeking?** All of us—it's practically a definition of human nature!
- **Who rejects the truth (see 1 v 18-21)?** All of us—we live in God's creation, but we have all spent a large part of our lives failing to glorify our Creator as God, or giving thanks to him.
- **Who does evil (see 2 v 1)?** All of us—none of us can judge others as bad because we are all guilty of doing the same things

7.
The righteous will receive eternal life (v 7) and glory, honour and peace (v 10). The righteous are those 'who by persistence in doing good seek glory, honour and immortality' (v 7). There is an apparent contradiction between verse 7 and what we learned last session. Paul appears to say that 'good' people will go to heaven. The key word to focus on here is 'persist' (see follow-up questions below). Assuming Paul does not contradict himself, this category of person consists of no one, except Jesus Christ. Nobody else consistently does good, and hence everyone falls into the category of 'trouble and distress'.

- **Who defines what is good?** God, as discussed in Session 2, question 4. Before we label ourselves as 'good' we need to know what God thinks is good.
- **What does it mean to persist in doing good?** The dictionary defines 'persist' as 'to continue firmly or obstinately in doing something, even if people criticise you or try to persuade you to give up. Doing something good now and again is not enough to make us righteous.
- **Where should we seek 'glory, honour and immortality' (v 6)?** (he word 'immortality' tells us that we can seek these things only from God. Righteousness is not just a matter of doing good things, but of being in a right relationship with God. Notice also, in 3 v 11 and 18, that sin is not just a matter of doing bad things, but of ignoring and dishonouring God.

8. Paul's conclusion is that everyone is under sin. 2 v 7 is true—God will give eternal life to anyone who qualifies as righteous. But the fact of the matter is that only one person has ever qualified—Jesus Christ. Everyone else fails to qualify.

9. The desire for justice is common to all cultures, classes, and ages of human beings. Just think of how early in life a child will complain that 'It's not fair'.

- True justice is not possible in this world, because judges can't find out the truth perfectly, can't see the secrets of people's hearts, and are themselves sinners, affected to a greater or lesser degree by factors such as prejudice, self-interest and wrong motives.
- Only God can give true justice, because only God knows everything and is completely perfect. However, people generally dislike the idea that God will judge everyone. The problem is that

there can be no justice in the universe without God's judgment. We need to understand that judgment is good because it shows God cares.

10. Think about it: This is the most important question in the course. Make sure you all spend time on it. After a minute or so of thinking, each person can have the opportunity to answer the question—a simple yes or no, without discussion at this stage. When everyone has answered, the two answers can be challenged.

- **If the answer is No**—do we really want an arbitrary God who isn't interested in justice? Surely that would mean that God could treat us unjustly, show favouritism, disregard the truth etc—the opposite of all the things we learnt about his judgment in question 4.
- **If the answer is Yes**—God will judge each of us and we will all be condemned.

This is the gospel dilemma—how can God be just and, at the same time, how can we be saved from his judgment? We all need to feel the weight of this 'Catch 22' situation.

REVIEW

This passage shows how we all qualify as unrighteous, and therefore, all face God's punishment on the Day of Judgment. But is there a glimmer of hope in verse 4? Paul mentions God's kindness, tolerance and patience, which should lead us towards repentance. The point of these remarks however, which are addressed to so-called 'good' people who think they are better than others, is that the opportunity presented by God's kindness is completely squandered. 'Good' people won't accept that they are not truly good. Instead, they stubbornly refuse to repent, making their guilt and final punishment worse (2 v 5). What looks like a glimmer of hope is, in fact, no help at all. There is nothing in this session that can help anyone to be saved from God's wrath and judgment.

PRAY

'Have mercy on me, O God, according to your unfailing love; according to your great compassion blot out my transgressions... Against you, you only, have I sinned and done what is evil in your sight, so that you are proved right when you speak and justified when you judge.' **Psalm 51 v 4**

Think about the following questions to guide you in closing the session with a prayer.

- What do we deserve from God, and what do we need?
- How should we pray?

EXPLORE MORE

What's the same?

- Jesus teaches that unrighteous people will be subject to judgment.
- Jesus teaches that people are judged unrighteous, not just because of wrong acts, but even for wrong thoughts (compare 'men's secrets'— 2 v 16).

What else do we learn?

- Jesus describes the punishment of the unrighteous as 'the fire of hell'.
- Jesus' standards of righteousness are far more stringent than those of past or current religious leaders.

4

Romans 2 v 17-29 and 3 v 19-20
WHAT CAN RELIGION DO?

THE BIG IDEA

Religion (even God's religion—the law of Moses) can't solve the problem of sin.

THE ISSUES

1. This session implicitly draws the distinction between 'religion' and Christianity. Religion is about appeasing God or 'gods' or fate by doing good things. Even non-religious people are 'religious' in this way—they live a good life, are nice, treat their family well etc.

2. People will be split over this session—some will consider it good news, since they have been oppressed with religion in the past; others will struggle with letting go of their own good actions as their reason for believing that they please God, or feeling good about themselves.

SUMMARY

Having understood the facts of our sinfulness and God's coming judgment, people tend to respond by throwing themselves into pleasing God—renewing their efforts to be more disciplined about going to church, praying, giving to charity, helping neighbours, giving up bad habits, reading the Bible etc. In other words, turning to religion to overcome the problem of sin. No one relied more than the Jews on the rituals and rules of God's law to save themselves from God's wrath. Paul speaks to them in Romans 2 v 17-29, but it's more bad news for them, and us!

Notice how central God's law is to the lives of the Jews—they rely on it (v 17); they are instructed by it (v 18); they teach it to others (v 19-20); they brag about it (v 23). But despite all this, and most critically, they break God's law (v 23-24). All this teaching of God's law only results in exposing them as utter hypocrites (v 21-23), to the utter dishonour of God's name (v 24).

The most fundamental mark of Jewish faith and identity was circumcision. Without this, you couldn't enjoy any other privileges and responsibilities set out in the law. Only if a man was circumcised could he call himself a Jew—ie: one of God's people—and enter the temple to make gifts and offerings to God. Circumcision had become shorthand for 'being righteous'. So imagine the shock when Paul tells his readers that if they break the law, God will consider them uncircumcised (v 25). Even worse, an uncircumcised man who keeps the law will be accepted by God as one of his people (v 26-27)! God isn't interested in outward physical marks (v 28), but in our hearts—have they been changed by the Holy Spirit to be pleasing to God? (v 29)?

Paul's conclusion in chapter 3 v 19-20 is that no one will be declared righteous in God's sight by trying to keep the law—even God's own law; it only makes us conscious of our sin. The challenge of this session is to understand that doing 'good' things or religious rituals will never make us righteous, and so will never save us from God's judgment. In fact, there is nothing we can do at all to help ourselves.

GUIDANCE ON QUESTIONS

1. This question deals with belief systems ranging from the major world religions to local tribal religions that aim to appease spirits. It can be answered both from an outsider's and an insider's point of view. For instance, an outsider, such as a sociologist, might view religion as a means of social control or a way of building up community identity. This is fine, but we are really interested in what a religion itself thinks its purpose is, and how it believes it can help people to relate to God. Find out what thinking is common to all types of religion. This will reveal that the purpose of religion in general is doing things to find favour with God. Think about questions such as:

- **In what ways do religious people live differently to non-religious people?** They act to do what a god or spirit thinks is good, rather than just following their own ideas.
- **What sorts of things do religious people do?** They practise rituals, learn teaching, give gifts, make sacrifices and follow rules.
- **Who decides what religious people should do?** The god or spirit of the religion, or their human spokesperson eg: priest, witchdoctor etc.
- **Why do religious people do religious things?** They hope to be rewarded by the god or spirit of the religion because they are doing things that please them.

2. God requires that people keep, or 'observe' his law (see 2 v 25; also look back at 2 v 13). The Jews had failed to keep God's law, as can be seen from the series of rhetorical questions in v 21-23, which imply that they did the very things they were preaching against. See also the conclusion in v 24.

3. The point of this question is to see how Jewish religious life was deeply involved with the law. The Jews relied on God's law to give them a special relationship with him (v 17); they were instructed by it (v 18); they taught it to others (v 19-20); they bragged about it (v 23). But none of their devotion to the law was good enough, because they failed at the critical point by breaking the law.

4. The condemned law-breaker in verse 27 is a Jew, ie: someone who has been circumcised and who has God's law—in other words, someone who believes that he has all the right qualifications to be accepted as one of God's people. Paul's Jewish readers may hardly have been able to believe their ears! Paul was overturning centuries of 'received wisdom'—the belief that all Jews, because they were circumcised and had God's law, were the people of God, and that everyone else was not.

5. It isn't circumcision, but obeying God's law that makes a person right with God (v 25). Circumcision is like a degree certificate—if you have studied at university and passed your exams, your certificate is worth something, but if you have never studied the course or taken the exams, the certificate is completely worthless.

6. Think about it: Baptism, confirmation, church-going, confession, going to Mass or communion, giving to the needy, meditation, retreats, vigils, fasting, pilgrimages etc. are all religious practices which people hope will make them acceptable to God. People do these things in a compartment of their lives labelled 'religious stuff' or 'pleasing God', and then go and live the rest of their lives (as workers, consumers, members of a family, residents of a community etc.), perhaps without even thinking about God, let alone allowing those 'non-religious' areas of their lives to be affected by what he has said.

7. No one will be declared righteous by observing the law (3 v 20).

8. The law makes us conscious of sin (3 v 20).

9. Note that Paul is talking about God's law, given through Moses to the people of Israel, after they had been rescued by God from slavery in Egypt. There is nothing wrong with God's law—the problem is with us.

10. Think about it: This question often reveals fuzzy thinking, in Christians as well as non-Christians. The question is deliberately ambiguous in order to expose that fuzzy thinking. People will often answer that reading the Bible, praying, singing, the Lord's Supper etc. (in other words, religious duties) will bring us closer to God. This reveals a human way of thinking ie: the problem = 'far away' from God; the solution = a process of getting closer to him. But actually, the problem is that we all start off, not just far away from God, but *enemies of God,* effectively dead as regards any contact or relationship with him. Religious duties cannot be steps on the way to God because we are dead in our sin. Doing religious things is just like putting nice clothes on a corpse!

We have the problem that our sin must be judged by the God who is just, and we need something to solve that problem. Hence the second part of the question. When any religious practice is suggested as a way of getting us closer to God, we need to ask: does it solve the problem of sin? Reading the Bible, praying, and going to church may help us to understand God, ourselves and the problem of sin, but none of that changes the fact that God must punish each of us for our sin.

What about people who say they have 'experienced God' in singing, for instance? We need to understand how easy it is to misinterpret a feeling as an experience of God. The reality, clearly taught in God's Word, is that, whether I feel it or not, God is angry at my sin. That issue has to be sorted before anything else.

REVIEW

Could the uncircumcised person who obeys the law, mentioned in v 27, possibly show us how to be righteous? The question is, can there be anyone like this? As we saw in Session 2, Paul concludes that everyone—Jew and Gentile—is under sin. The point in v 27 is that it is not circumcision but obedience that God requires of us. To make sure his readers get this, he emphasises it in a hypothetical but shockingly memorable way.

Verse 29 describes a person who would be praised, not condemned, by God—someone who has received circumcision of the heart, by the Spirit. Notice that this isn't something *we* can do—it is done by God's Spirit. Nor are we told how we can get this circumcision of the heart. So, we have learned nothing in this session that can help us to be righteous. How about some homework for next session?

People might appreciate the opportunity to have a go at answering question 2 in Session Five at home, in preparation for the next Bible study. Remember— good news is coming at last!

PRAY

'You do not delight in sacrifice, or I would bring it; you do not take pleasure in burnt offerings. The sacrifices of God are a broken spirit; a broken and contrite heart, O God, you will not despise.'
Psalm 51v 16-17.

Think about this question to guide you in closing the session with a prayer.

- How should we come to God, and how should we not come, when we pray?

EXPLORE MORE

Encourage the group to do the Explore More section as homework. Also encourage them to answer for themselves question 2 of Session 5.

Isaiah 1 v 10-17

God hated the religious practices of the Jews and wanted no contact with these people—'I have more than enough of burnt offerings...I have no pleasure in the blood of bulls...' (v 11); 'Stop bringing meaningless offerings! Your incense is detestable to me...I cannot bear your evil assemblies.' (v 12); 'your appointed feasts my soul hates. They have become a burden to me. I am weary of bearing them.' (v 14); 'I will hide my eyes from you...I will not listen.' (v 15). The reason for God's disgust was that the Jews only bothered about performing the rituals specified in the law (sacrifices, feasts, prayers), but they failed to keep God's laws about doing right, being just and compassionate.

What's the same?

- God is not interested in empty religious rituals.
- God wants people to obey his law.

What else do we learn?

- God is passionate, both in his hatred of religious pretence, and in his justice and compassion.
- God longs for his people to be made right (v 16-17).

5 Romans 3 v 21-31
GOD'S GIFT

THE BIG IDEA

The atoning death of Jesus alone can save us from our sin and its consequences.

THE ISSUES

1. If you have managed to keep the studies focused, this will be the first time that Jesus and salvation have been discussed.

2. When considering Jesus' death in our place to pay the penalty that our sins deserve (substitutionary atonement), it is worth thinking about what would be required for someone to be able to take the sins of every person.

i) someone who had no sin of their own and hence, deserved no judgment.
ii) someone who had an infinite capacity to take sin—ie: God.

Use an illustration about bank accounts. Our account is deeply in the red, but Jesus not only takes on our debt, but also credits our account with his wealth!

SUMMARY

A note about Romans 3 v 1-8, not included in this course: Everyone is shocked at the conclusions Paul has reached by the end of Romans 3, no one more so than his Jewish readers. If circumcision and knowledge of God's own law do not make people righteous and acceptable to God, what is the advantage in being a Jew? Paul addresses this question in 3v 1-8, before reaching the conclusion that we have already looked at in 3 v 9-20: all of us, whether we are Jewish or not, are sinners, and God's law cannot help us—it only makes us conscious of our sin.

So now, if even God's law cannot help us to become righteous and save us from God's wrath, what hope is there for us? Absolutely none! There is not one thing that any of us can do to save ourselves. This is the ultimate bad news.

At which point, we are finally ready to hear the good news. We cannot do anything to become righteous, but God has already done something. Righteousness comes from God (v 21); and we have been told about this righteousness in God's written Word (v 21); it comes to us through faith in Jesus Christ (v 22); it is for all who believe, whether Jew or Gentile, because all have sinned and all need God's help (v 23); God justifies us—declares us 'not guilty' when we believe in Jesus Christ (v 24); this justification is free and by grace—we cannot pay for it and we do not deserve it (v 24); Jesus has redeemed us—he has paid the price that God required in order to set us free from our slavery to sin and judgment (v 24); Jesus' death wasn't just a tragic end to a good life—it was God's plan that Jesus would be a sacrifice of atonement, dying in our place, taking the penalty of our sin, turning aside God's wrath against us onto himself (v 25—see NIV footnote), so that we could be reconciled to God; in doing all this God has shown that he is both just (he punishes all sin) and is also the one who justifies (declares 'not guilty') any sinner who has faith in Jesus (v 25-26). Those who believe in Jesus can never boast about their salvation, because it has all been done by God (v 27-28).

The challenge of this session is for each of us to repent of trusting in our 'goodness' or anything we do to make us righteous, and to put our faith in Jesus and what he has done instead.

GUIDANCE ON QUESTIONS

1. A true gift (not one that is expected eg: by a host/hostess) is undeserved, and there is no obligation on the giver to give anything. So someone who receives a gift that is unexpected and undeserved ought to feel a debt of gratitude towards the giver and be inspired to similar generosity. On the other hand, a payment, right or reward is deserved in some way, and people expect to receive these things eg: an employer has an obligation to pay his workers; a client is expected to pay someone who provides goods or a service; a court of law is obliged to recognise a person's right; our society expects heroic deeds, outstanding achievements, loyalty and committed service etc. to be rewarded. We feel satisfied when we receive these things but not warm and grateful in the way that we feel when we have received a wonderful gift. Some people dislike accepting gifts because they don't want to owe a 'debt' of gratitude to someone else. In some situations this wariness is understandable (eg: a new 'date' paying for a meal, a competition judge receiving a gift from a competitor). Sometimes however, people are simply proud and mistrustful, and they end up missing out on the joys of warm, generous relationships.

2. No one will be declared righteous in God's sight.

3. It is probably best to discuss the bulleted questions first. This exercise could be quite stressful for some people, especially if they are not students. Hopefully, people might have written the summary as homework. However, allocating additional time during the session for people to work out a summary in pairs will help those who didn't do it as homework. How about also reading out a couple of other versions or paraphrases of the passage eg: The Message? Depending on the group, people's summaries could be read by the group leader, either privately or aloud, to check that all the teaching packed into these verses has been truly understood.

- **v 21-22:** People need righteousness. This comes from God, not from anything that we do. We get this righteousness by having faith (trusting) in Jesus Christ.
- **v 24:** 'Justified' is a word that comes from the law courts. God declares those who have faith in Jesus to be righteous, or 'not guilty' of sin.
- **v 24:** 'Grace' means 'undeserved favour or kindness'. We are totally undeserving of this righteousness from God, so we have no right to expect that God will do anything for us. There is nothing that we can do to earn it beforehand or pay for it afterwards.
- **v 24:** 'Redemption' is a word that comes from the marketplace. In the Old Testament, people were sometimes sold into slavery, as a 'last resort' means of

paying off their debts. If this happened to a Jew, members of his family were obliged to raise enough money to buy him back from the slave owner, a procedure known as redemption. Jesus Christ paid the price of his own life when he died on the cross, to free us from our slavery to sin and judgment.

- **v 25:** 'Atonement' is a word that comes from the temple. It means to pay a penalty and make amends for wrongdoing, so that there can be reconciliation between the wrongdoer and God. Every year, Israel kept the Day of Atonement, when the high priest would enter the most holy place in the temple with the blood of an animal that had been killed, and offer it to God as atonement for the sins of his people. But the New Testament tells us that these annual sacrifices were only copies of the true atoning sacrifice—Jesus Christ (see Hebrews 9 v 1-14 and 24-28). When Jesus died, it was not an unexpected tragedy, but the culmination of the plan of God. As he died, Jesus paid the penalty for human sin, making amends on behalf of sinners (see Mark 15 v 33-34 and 37-39). Because of the death of Jesus, sinful people can be reconciled to God.
- **v 25:** We need to have faith in Jesus' blood to get right with God. That means that we need to put our trust in the death of Jesus and what he achieved on the cross, to save us from God's judgment.

4. People need to clearly understand the following terms—justification, redemption and sacrifice of atonement—and how they relate to the death of Jesus Christ on the cross. It's good to illustrate these words by placing them within their original settings (see notes for question 3 above).

- **Justification**—Christ's death on the cross makes us 'not guilty' in the eyes of the law because the punishment for our sin has already been paid. This means we can go free.
- **Redemption**—Christ's death was sufficient payment of the price required to buy us out of slavery to sin and its consequences. This means we can be restored into God's family.
- **Sacrifice of atonement**—This term comes from the temple practice of sacrificing a lamb. The idea was that the lamb suffered the punishment for the sin of the one bring the sacrifice. This means that God's right and just anger is deflected onto the 'lamb', in our case Jesus. This is great news that we should delight in.

5. God is showing that he is a just God by judging sin. He can't just ignore it. Until the time of Jesus' death on the cross, all the sins committed before the time of Jesus had gone unpunished (see 3 v 25). Until Jesus' death, people could rightly accuse God of failing to be just. But when Jesus died on the cross, God exacted from him the fearful penalty that all those sins had deserved; at that point, the terrible cost of every hurt and wrong committed against another person was paid by Jesus, and justice was done.

6. Think about it: This is the most important question to ask when investigating a religion or belief about God. Many claim that God is both just and merciful, but the question is: **how can he punish all wrongdoing and, at the same time, let wrongdoers go free?** The answer is only at the cross of Jesus Christ.

- People may have various ideas about how God might be both just and merciful, which can be discussed at this point. But remember the conclusions reached so far on this course: everyone is guilty of sin; if God is just he must punish every sin; God's righteous decree demands that sin is punished by death.
- Many people believe that all religions have part of the truth; each will lead you along a different path, but to the same end. But the Christian good news is opposite to other religions. In Session 4, we learned that no religious duty can solve the problem of our sin. Unlike other religions, Christianity teaches that we cannot seek to please God by things that we do. Righteousness is something that comes from God, through faith in Jesus, and a Christian is someone who trusts that God, through Jesus Christ, will save them from sin and judgment. Can we do things to please God (as other religions say), or is it true that no one does good and no one seeks God (as Christianity teaches)? Only one of those views can be right.

  The Christian good news is also unique. Only in the cross of Jesus Christ can God be both perfectly just and merciful. No other religion shows how God can do that. Therefore, if Christianity is right, other religions must be wrong.

Key sign of a true Christian—they are convinced that Jesus Christ is the only way to God.

7. God's gift of righteousness is not deserved—it comes 'freely by his grace' (v 24). Imagine your copy of Romans stopped short at the beginning of 3 v 24—'for all have sinned and fall short of the glory of God and are...' What would you imagine comes next? Which one of us would ever guess that it is the words 'justified freely by his grace'?

8. 'All who believe' receive this righteousness (v 22) and they receive it by faith in Jesus Christ or faith in his blood (v 22, 25, 28, 30). Today the word 'faith' is often misunderstood to mean all kinds of mystical and religious things, and the danger is that we turn faith itself into a good work. We need to understand that faith is trust in what God has done for us, and therefore, true faith gives up any dependence on what 'I do'. Everybody has faith—either in themselves or in God. True faith looks at the thing or person being trusted, not at itself. Someone bringing a lamb to the temple placed their hands on the animal to symbolise the fact that their sin was transferred to the lamb; then they had faith that the lamb's death was a substitute for their punishment.

9. Those who believe in Jesus can never boast about how clever or right they were to become a Christian, because they have contributed nothing—it has all been done by God (v 27-28). 'Believing in Jesus' means trusting that he has done everything needed to make us righteous and save us from God's judgment. Nor, for the same reasons, should they look down on those who have not become Christians, and feel that they are more stupid or more wicked than themselves.

Key sign of a true Christian—someone who will always admit that they are a sinner, and readily accepts that they are worse than others.

10. Think about it: If people try to impress God with what they have done and how good they have been, they will find that they are too sinful for God to forgive; if God is just he must punish all their sin and every sin. But no one is too sinful for God to forgive, if they come trusting in Jesus and what he did on the cross to save sinners. It isn't about anything we have done, however good or bad or utterly evil we may have been—it's about what Jesus has done on our behalf, so whether we have lived like a saint or a genocidal tyrant makes no difference.

Key sign of a true Christian—someone who accepts that even someone like Hitler can be forgiven by God if they trust in Jesus Christ to save them.

PRAY

In this session, a prayer has been included in the Study Guide. Not everyone may be ready to pray this for themselves yet, but it is still useful for everyone to have the opportunity of seeing the kind of words that people have often used when they reach the point of putting their faith in Jesus Christ to save them from sin. Anyone who prays this prayer for themselves should be encouraged to tell the group leader or a Christian friend.

EXPLORE MORE

- **Exodus 12 v 1-13:** The people of Israel were saved from God's judgment by taking the blood of a lamb that had been killed, and painting it on the doorframe of their houses.
- **Isaiah 53 v 4-12:** God's servant is punished by God (v 4) for our sins (v 5, 6, 8, 11, 12). The result is peace and healing (v 5) and justification (v 11) for us, even though we have all done wrong (v 6), whereas God's servant suffers oppression and judgment (v 8) and death (v 9), although he had done nothing wrong (v 9). But it was the plan of God that, by dying, his servant would become a guilt offering for us (v10). In this prophecy, we see that the role of the lamb in Exodus 12 is taken by God's servant.
- **John 1 v 29:** John tells us that Jesus is the Lamb of God, who takes away the sin of the world. Jesus is the servant prophesied in Isaiah, and he is the true sacrifice that will save us from God's judgment, of which the lamb in Exodus 12 was only a copy.

6

Romans 5 v 1-11

RIGHT WITH GOD

THE BIG IDEA

Those who put their faith in Jesus Christ have wonderful blessings in him.

THE ISSUES

1. Christian confidence: A central theme of this session is our confidence in Christ that the achievements of Jesus' death will hold good for us on the Day of Judgment. How certain can we be of going to heaven? If God was willing to send Jesus to die for us when we were his enemies, won't he come through when it comes to completing the deal (salvation)? Of course He will! Christians have the (humble) right to be sure of their place in heaven precisely because we have not contributed anything to it—Jesus has done it all.

2. Christian growth: This session shows how the Christian good news can completely and wonderfully transform the lives—past, present and future— of those who put their trust in Jesus Christ. But we need to remember that Christians continue to live in a world affected by sin and are not automatically protected from tough experiences. Christians have already been wonderfully saved, but there is more to come.

3. A new life: For those who prayed the prayer at the end of Session Five, this will be their welcome to a new life as forgiven children of God. Others will still be on the 'outside, looking in'. This session brings everything together and helps people count the personal cost of not becoming a Christian.

SUMMARY

At last we have had the good news—God, who is both merciful and just, can make sinners righteous (3 v 21–31). When this happens nothing can ever be the same. Christians have been justified (v 1, 9) and reconciled to God (v 10, 11). Instead of being under God's wrath, they have gained access into grace—they experience God's wonderful kindness that they do not deserve (v 2). Christians now have peace with God (v 1), hope (v 5) and joy (v 3, 11). Even though they still suffer in this life (v 3), they can rejoice. They can be certain that, because of Christ's death, they are loved by God (v 8) and that he uses their sufferings to increase their perseverance, mature their characters and strengthen their hope (v 3-4).

But what of the future? The Day of Judgment has not yet come. Can Christians be absolutely sure that they will be saved from God's wrath on that day? The answer is found in the resurrection of Jesus. The resurrection shows that Jesus' death achieved its purpose in paying the penalty of our sin so that we could be justified and forgiven (4 v 25). The resurrection also means that Jesus is now alive. If so much was achieved by his death—his suffering and 'weakness' making possible our justification and reconciliation to God (v 9, 10)— now that he is living and powerful, we can be confident that his plans will be completed, and we shall be saved on the Day of Judgment.

The challenge of this session is for those who have put their faith in Jesus Christ, to live in the light of that, confident of God's love, rejoicing in suffering and certain that they will be finally saved from God's wrath, and live with him in heaven. And for those who have not trusted in Jesus, to confront the reasons why not.

A note about Romans 4, not included in this course: An illustration about Abraham in chapter 4 has been skipped. Paul spends time showing his Jewish readers that even Abraham, the 'father of the Jews' was not justified because of anything he had done, but through faith—he 'believed God' (4 v 3).

GUIDANCE ON QUESTIONS

1. It may be, as often happens, that no one can think of any examples of reconciliation, which only goes to show what a rare, and remarkable thing this is.

2. Often, people are not sure whether a phrase like 'we have been justified' (v 1) goes in the past or present column. Actually, 'have been justified' is neither past nor present—it's present perfect, indicating a past event or action with present relevance (we have been justified = we are justified now). For the purposes of this question, all actions or events phrased as 'have been' or 'has done' should be listed in the 'past' column:

PAST

- justified (v 1, 9)
- gained access into grace (v 2)
- God has poured out his love into our hearts (v 5)
- given the Holy Spirit (v 5)
- Christ died for the ungodly/for us (v 6, 8)
- reconciled to God (v 10, 11)

PRESENT

- have peace with God (v 1)
- rejoice…
  - …in our hope (v 2)
  - …in sufferings (v 3)
  - …in God (v 11)
- have hope (v 2, 5)

FUTURE

- will be saved from God's wrath (v 9, 10)

3. Think about it: Often, people don't seem to have thought about this question before. The group should discuss how their thinking would change (for instance, about the future). What would become important in their lives? What would they want to change? The key thing is that their life would change radically.

- **Thinking**—for example: God is no longer your angry Judge but your generous loving Father; you are no longer a 'decent person' but a sinner saved by grace; Jesus is no longer a distant figure of history but your Lord and Master, to whom you owe everything; the future is no longer scary but full of hope etc.
- **Life**—for example: you no longer live to please yourself, but to show your thankfulness and love to God, who has forgiven you, and Jesus, who has saved you; you will want other people to know this good news; when suffering comes you can trust God and be confident of

his love for you; you won't be making your home in this world, but looking forward to eternal life with your heavenly Father; you will be able to forgive others because you know how much God has forgiven you etc.

A Key sign of a true Christian—someone who knows that their life has been changed by the good news of Jesus Christ; so, someone who has *become* a Christian, rather than someone who has 'always been a Christian'.

4. By faith (v 2). When we trust in Jesus to do everything needed to make us righteous, God no longer acts towards us in judgment (treating us as we deserve), but in grace (treating us with kindness and love which we don't deserve). The question is will we, in all circumstances, trust that God is treating us in grace, not judgment?

5. When people suffer they tend to think that it is because God is judging them for some particular sin. They imagine that if God really loved them he would not let them suffer. But v 3 shows that those who have been justified will still have sufferings. In other words, suffering or freedom from suffering is no indication of whether a person is right with God or not.

6. Christians are allowed by God to suffer, because through their sufferings he can do something good that otherwise would not happen. Suffering produces the ability to persevere, and the experience that God always 'comes through' for his people. This cultivates a strong character that is able to trust God come what may, because of the experience of God's faithfulness in times of trouble. Such a person is able to fix their eyes on the future hope of wonderful eternal life with God, rather than investing all their energies in this temporary and disappointing life. Notice that God doesn't leave Christians to suffer without resources to help them—he has given them the Holy Spirit (v 5).

These questions on suffering may seem out of place, but it is helpful to discuss that Christianity is a hard way of life, that Christians still suffer, but that we have a hope of something more than this world. The topic of evangelism is worth raising, since the truth of the gospel is not always welcome in the west and so suffering of some sort should be expected. For some international folk, this topic is particularly important since they may well suffer physically, emotionally or culturally if they become Christians.

7. God has demonstrated his love for us in sending Jesus Christ to die for us (v 8). When suffering comes, Christians don't need to question whether God still loves them. God's love is not shown in giving someone an easy life; as we have seen, God allows Christians to suffer precisely because that is the way in which he can do something good in their lives. Instead, God's love is shown in the cross of Jesus Christ. If Christians are questioning whether God really loves them, they need to remind themselves of the cross because that is what demonstrates God's love for his people. If we think that our circumstances demonstrate whether God loves us or not, we will never be certain of his love because circumstances always change. But because the cross of Jesus Christ is an unalterable fact of history, Christians can always have great confidence that God loves them.

8. Christians will be saved from God's wrath (v 9).

9. Romans 4 v 25 tells us that while it was the death of Jesus that paid the penalty for our sin, it was his resurrection that ensured we could be justified. It's important for us to understand that the death and resurrection of Christ are inseparable. Because of the resurrection, we can see that God has accepted Jesus' payment for our sin, which means that sinners can be justified through Christ, and there is no longer any need for him to remain dead.

10. Think about it: This question should lead into a review of what has been learned about salvation over the whole course. Christians can be absolutely certain that they will go to heaven instead of being punished by God on the Day of Judgment. Some people believe it is very arrogant to think like this. That's because they still wrongly think that whether or not someone goes to heaven depends on how they have lived; how can such a person ever be sure that they have lived a good enough life to get into heaven?
But, as we saw in Session 5, getting into heaven does not depend on how we have lived, but on the fact that Jesus Christ was punished in our place for our sins.
A Christian can be certain of going to heaven because, although they are a complete sinner, they are saved by the death of Jesus Christ.

Key sign of a true Christian—someone who is certain that they are going to heaven, because of what Jesus Christ has done.

PRAY

'To him who is able to keep you from falling and to present you before his glorious presence without fault and with great joy—to the only God our Saviour be glory, majesty, power and authority, through Jesus Christ our Lord, before all ages, now and for evermore! Amen.'
Jude v 25

Think about the following question to guide you in closing the session with a prayer.

- How will we pray differently when we come to God through faith in Jesus Christ?

At the end of the course, you might think it appropriate to encourage the group to think of something

- to thank God for
- to say sorry for
- to ask from him.

CONCLUSION

Having completed these studies, people will be at different stages in their understanding of the gospel and their response to it. So what next? Often, groups like these form strong friendships, and people want to stay together to study more of the Bible. Whether or not your group members have prayed a prayer of commitment, their first need is to continue being taught the truths of the Bible. Suggested options are:

- You could suggest that the group does a further course, like *Christianity Explored,* looking at the life and teaching of Jesus Christ. This is something that they could invite others to as well.
- You could encourage your group to join you at a regular church meeting, if it is

accessible to newcomers (ie: the teaching is clear and from the Bible, and they will not be expected to do anything that will embarrass or confuse them.)

- For those who are convinced of the truth of Romans 1-5, and want to become Christians, how about encouraging them to pray, either with another Christian or alone, something along the lines of the prayer at the end of session 5? A further course that investigates the life and teaching of Jesus Christ, or a beginner's guide to living as a Christian would be helpful.
- If you are able, you could offer to do one-to-one Bible study with anyone who is interested. (See *One to One* by Sophie Peace for more help with this. Available from The Good Book Company.)

EXPLORE MORE

What's the same?

- In all things (including suffering), God works for the good of those who love him (v 28).
- A Christian's confidence of God's love is based on the fact that he sent Jesus Christ to die for sinners (v 32).
- Suffering cannot separate Christians from God's love (v 35).

What else do we learn?

- God predestined Christians to be made like Jesus (v 29).
- The risen Lord Jesus is interceding with God for Christians (v 34).
- Nothing in all creation will be able to separate Christians from the love of God in Christ Jesus (v 38-39).